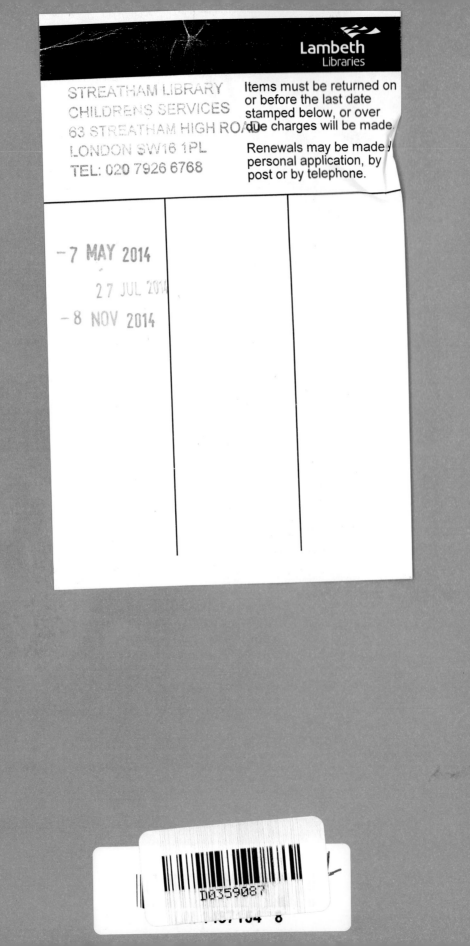

FIRST
SPORT

FOOTBALL

James Nixon

Photography by Bobby Humphrey

W

FRANKLIN WATTS
LONDON•SYDNEY

First published in 2014
by Franklin Watts

Franklin Watts
338 Euston Road
London NW1 3BH

Franklin Watts Australia
Level 17/207 Kent Street
Sydney, NSW 2000

Series Editor: Julia Bird
Planning and production by Discovery Books Ltd
Editor: James Nixon
Series designer: Ian Winton
Commissioned photography: Bobby Humphrey
Picture credits: Shutterstock: pp. 2 (muszy), 3 & 19 top (muzsy),
4 (muzsy), 5 (muzsy), 6 top (Nancy Hixson), 6 bottom (muzsy),
7 top and cover (muzsy), 7 bottom (Olga Dmitrieva), 8 (Natursports),
10 (muzsy), 11 (muzsy), 14 (muzsy), 15 bottom (muzsy), 16 (muzsy),
17 (muzsy), 21 top (Maxisport), 21 bottom (Barone Firenze),
22 top (Sirikorn Techatraibhop), 23 top (Petur Asgeirsson).

The author, packager and publisher would like to thank Leominster
Minors Football Club for their help and participation in this book.

Dewey number 796.3'34
ISBN: 978 1 4451 2632 6
Library ebook ISBN: 978 1 4451 2636 4

Printed in China

Franklin Watts is a division of Hachette Children's Books,
an Hachette UK company.
www.hachette.co.uk

Contents

The aim of the game

Football is the most popular sport in the world. A football match is played between two teams of 11 players. To win a match, one team must score more goals than the other.

OPPONENT a person who is on the opposite team in a game

Goals are scored in a net at each end of the pitch. In play, only the goalkeeper can handle the ball. Players are not allowed to trip, push or pull their **opponents**.

Get kitted out

The most important piece of kit for a footballer is a pair of boots that fit properly. Football boots have **studs** on the bottom to stop you slipping. Players also wear shinpads to protect their legs.

Shinpads

Boot

Stud

STUDS
metal or plastic knobs fixed on to the base of a boot, to provide better grip

The teams playing each other wear different coloured **strips.**

STRIP the set of clothes worn by a footballer

Goalkeepers wear different colours from the other players. They also have gloves to handle the ball.

Scoring goals

To score goals you need to be good at shooting.

You can place the ball into the corner of the net with the side of your foot. Or you can beat the goalkeeper by kicking the ball with power.

Good **strikers** can score all types of goals.

They sometimes **volley** or head the ball into the net.

STRIKER
a player on a football team whose job is to score goals

VOLLEY
kick the ball before it touches the ground

9

Keeping the ball

A footballer should not give the ball to the other team. You need to keep the ball under control. If the ball bounces away from you, an opponent will take it!

You can put your body in the way to stop opponents **tackling** you.

TACKLE
take the ball from an opponent

Short, accurate passes to other teammates are a good way to keep your team on the ball.

Teamwork

Passing is the best way to move your team towards the goal.

Players who do not have the ball need to run into space so that their teammate can pass the ball to them.

Deciding which teammate to pass to is an important skill. Short passing is safer. Sometimes there is a chance to make a longer, attacking pass.

A long pass into the **penalty box** is a good choice if there are strikers there to score.

PENALTY BOX the area in front of each goal where the goalkeeper can handle the ball

Dribbling

Players can move the ball up the pitch by running with the ball. This is called **dribbling**. Dribbling is risky. Only the most skilful players can dribble for long without losing the ball to an opponent.

DRIBBLE
take the ball past opponents with touches of the ball

Good dribblers use speed and clever tricks to get past their opponents.

You can push the ball through a player's legs and run past them. This is called a nutmeg.

Defending

Stopping goals is just as important as scoring them. When your opponents are attacking, it is time to defend. Defenders **mark** their opponents and challenge them for the ball.

MARK stay close to an opponent to stop them getting the ball

Defenders are very good at clearing the ball from danger. They make tackles to win the ball back.

To tackle, you can stay on your feet, or slide in to take the ball away. When you tackle, you must kick the ball and not your opponent.

Goalkeeping

It is up to the goalkeeper to keep the ball out of the net. They jump, stretch and dive to push the ball around the post or over the **crossbar.**

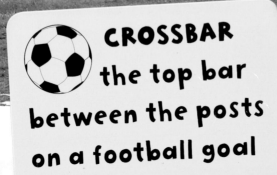

CROSSBAR
the top bar between the posts on a football goal

Goalkeepers must catch shots and long, high passes into their penalty area if they can.

Good goalkeepers are skilled at putting themselves in the right place. If they block most of the goal, it makes it harder for the attacker to score.

Throw-ins, corners and free kicks

If the ball is kicked across the outside line of the pitch, play is started again by the other team. They take a throw-in where the ball crossed the line.

If a player knocks the ball over the line behind their goal, the attackers are given a corner kick by the corner flag.

The referee runs the match. He or she blows a whistle for a **foul** if a player handles the ball or trips, pushes or kicks an opponent. The other side are given a free kick.

FOUL
an action which breaks the rules of the game

Free kicks are often great chances to score a goal.

Positions

Football teams play in a **formation**. In a formation each player has a different job.

Goalkeeper

Defenders

Midfielders

Strikers

FORMATION
the way the players are arranged on the pitch

Defenders need to be strong, good in the air and good at tackling.

Midfielders are very good at passing. They do a lot of running. Midfielders who play on the **wings** are often quick and good at dribbling.

WINGS
the parts of the pitch close to the sidelines

Strikers are skilled at beating defenders and putting the ball in the net!

Index